HILL BOSWELL'S
GREEN
TREASURY

Stories • Poems • Rhymes

CARNIVAL

Goldilocks and The Three Bears

There was once a little girl called Goldilocks who lived with her mother and father in a house near a wood. One bright summer morning. Goldilocks went into the wood to gather wild flowers. She had often been told not to wander too far away, but this morning she forgot. There always seemed to be lovelier flowers a little farther on. Presently she came to a cottage in a clearing.

"I wonder who lives there?" she said.

She was a very bold little girl. She walked straight up and knocked on the door. There was no answer, so she lifted the latch and walked in.

She was in the living-room, and on the table stood three bowls of porridge. A big bowl, a middle-size bowl, and a little bowl. The smell of the porridge made her feel hungry so she tasted a spoonful from the big bowl, but it was too hot. She tasted a spoonful from the middle-size bowl, but it was too cold. Then she tasted a spoonful from the little bowl and it was just right, so she ate up all the porridge.

Then she noticed three chairs. A big chair, a middle-size chair, and a little chair.

Goldilocks sat down on the big chair, but it was too hard. She sat down on the middle-size chair, but it was too soft. Then she sat down on the little chair and it felt just right, until *bang!* the bottom fell out!

Upstairs in the bedroom, Goldilocks saw three beds. A big bed, a middle-size bed, and a little bed. Suddenly she felt very sleepy and lay down on the big bed, but it was too hard. The middle-size bed was too soft, but the little bed was just right, and in no time at all Goldilocks was fast asleep.

Now, the cottage belonged to a family of bears who had gone out for a walk while their porridge cooled. When they got back, they knew that someone had been in the house.

"Who's been tasting *my* porridge?" growled Father Bear. "And *my* porridge?" cried Mother Bear. "*My* porridge is all eaten up!" squeaked Baby Bear.

Then the bears looked at their chairs.

"Who's been sitting in *my* chair?" growled Father Bear. "Who's been sitting in *my* chair?" cried Mother Bear.

"And who's been sitting in *my* chair and broken it!" squeaked Baby Bear.

Now the bears were very cross and went upstairs to look in their bedroom.

"Who's been lying on *my* bed?" growled Father Bear.

"And who's been lying on *my* bed?" cried Mother Bear.

"And look who's lying on *my* bed," squeaked Baby Bear. "It's a little girl!"

There lay Goldilocks, her head on Baby Bear's pillow.

"Well!" growled Father Bear. "Well!" cried Mother Bear. "Well!" squeaked Baby Bear.

The sound of their voices, all growling and crying and squeaking together, was so strange and so loud that Goldilocks heard it, even in her sleep, and she woke in a fright. She sat up in the little bear's bed and screamed at the sight of the three furry faces gazing at her.

"Poor thing!" said Mother Bear, patting her head gently with her big paw.

Goldilocks and the three bears went downstairs and out of the cottage. Father Bear showed her the way out of the wood and Mother Bear and Baby Bear waved goodbye until she was out of sight.

And Goldilocks never saw them again.

HUSH A BYE BABY

Hush-a-bye, baby,
  on the tree-top,
When the wind blows
  the cradle will rock;
When the bough breaks
  the cradle will fall,
And down will come baby,
  cradle and all.

The Jumblies

They went to sea in a Sieve, they did,
  In a Sieve they went to sea;
In spite of all their friends could say,
  On a winter's morn, on a stormy day,
In a Sieve they went to sea!

And when the Sieve turned round and round,
  And everyone cried: 'You'll all be drowned!'
They cried aloud: 'Our Sieve ain't big,
  But we don't care a button, we don't care a fig!
In a Sieve we'll go to sea!'

Far and few, far and few,
    Are the lands where the Jumblies live;
Their heads are green and their hands are blue,
    And they went to sea in a Sieve.

EDWARD LEAR

Diddle, Diddle Dumpling

Diddle, diddle, dumpling, my son John,
Went to bed with his trousers on;
One shoe off, and one shoe on,
Diddle, diddle, dumpling, my son John.

DOCTOR FOSTER

Doctor Foster went to Gloucester
In a shower of rain;
He stepped in a puddle,
Right up to his middle,
And never went there again.

Grasshopper Green

Grasshopper Green is a comical
                            chap;
  He lives on the best of fare.
Bright little trousers, jacket
                      and cap,
  These are his summer wear.

Out in the meadow he loves to go,
  Playing away in the sun;
It's hopperty, skipperty,
              high and low,
  Summer's the time for fun.

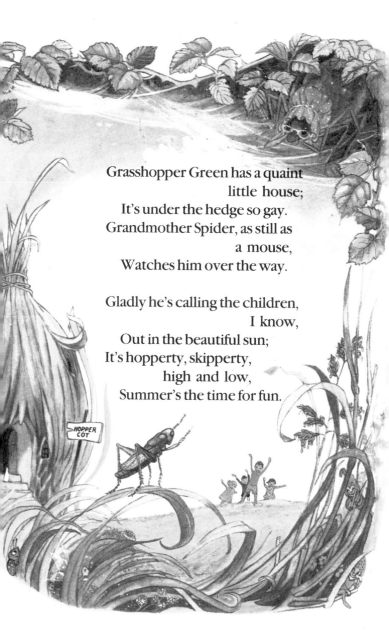

Grasshopper Green has a quaint
little house;
It's under the hedge so gay.
Grandmother Spider, as still as
a mouse,
Watches him over the way.

Gladly he's calling the children,
I know,
Out in the beautiful sun;
It's hopperty, skipperty,
high and low,
Summer's the time for fun.

HOPPER
COT

Georgie Porgie

Georgie Porgie, pudding and pie,
   Kissed the girls and made them cry.
When the boys came out to play,
   Georgie Porgie ran away.

CURLY LOCKS

Curly Locks! Curly Locks!
  Will you be mine?
You shall not wash dishes,
  Nor yet feed the swine;
But sit on a cushion,
  And sew a fine seam,
And feed upon strawberries,
  Sugar
      and
          cream.

The Winds
They Did Blow

The winds they did blow;
The leaves they did wag;
Along came a beggar boy,
And put me in his bag.

He took me up to London;
  A lady me did buy,
She put me in a silver cage,
  And hung me up on high.

With apples by the fire,
  And nuts for to crack,
Besides a little feather bed
  To rest my little back.

A ROBIN AND A ROBIN'S SON

A robin and a robin's son,
　　Once went to town to buy a bun,
They couldn't decide on plum or plain,
　　And so they went back home again.

The Pied Piper

This is the strange story of what happened a
long time ago in the old German town of
Hamelin.

Hamelin was as pleasant a town as you could
ever wish to live in. The houses, with their
crooked gables, leaned towards each other
across the street. The church spires rose high
above the tiled roofs, and outside the town wall
flowed the broad and shining River Weser.

Now whether it was because the harvest
that year had been an especially good one with
plenty of grain in the barns, or whether it was
because of the carelessness of the good people
of Hamelin who had enough food and to spare
in their larders, I do not know . . .

But one terrible year, the town found that it had been invaded by an army of rats. Life became a great misery for the people of Hamelin for the rats were everywhere, spoiling the food and terrifying the children. Rats in their beds and in their boots, in the cupboards and on the shelves, gnawing and scratching and squeaking. Brown rats, grey rats, black rats. Rats with fierce whiskers and rats with long tails. Young rats and old rats.

They scratched behind the walls, scurried about the kitchens, ran in and out of the houses, hundreds and thousands of them, all squeaking at the tops of their voices.

They killed the cats and fought the dogs. The people set traps but the rats were too clever to get caught.

The Hamelin
people grew so
worried that they
flocked to the town
hall and told the
mayor that he must
do something.

The mayor and the aldermen had been
sitting around the council table day after day,
worrying and arguing about nothing else but
RATS! But what *could* they do? The mayor
scratched his head and the treasurer did some
sums and the secretary wrote it all down, but
still they didn't know how to get rid of the rats.
As they sat fretting, there came a light rap on
the door, then the door opened gently and a
very strange figure entered.

The strangest thing about him was his long coat of different colours. The mayor thought he must be a strolling minstrel for he carried a musical pipe, holding it lovingly as though he longed to play.

He was tall and lean, and his appearance frightened the aldermen a little, but his smile was kind and his sharp eyes twinkled merrily as he walked up to the table.

"Please, your honours," he said softly, "I know a charm that will rid you of the rats."

"Who are you?" gasped the mayor.

"They call me the Pied Piper," he replied, and indeed, the name suited him. As he spoke, his fingers tapped on the pipe as if they itched to play. "My price is a thousand guilders," said the piper.

"*Fifty* thousand!" shouted the mayor. "No price is too high for a service like that!" He smiled at the treasurer and the treasurer nodded, and all the aldermen nodded.

"I ask for one thousand," murmured the Pied Piper. "A bargain is a bargain."

The Pied Piper stepped out into the street and raised the magic pipe to his lips. At the sound of the first note there was a pitter-patter on the cobblestones as out of the houses came the rats. The piper played a strange, eerie tune and the great army of rats followed him.

The noise of the scampering rats grew louder and louder, swelling to a tremendous roar as the thousands of rats tumbled out from every nook and cranny of the old town.

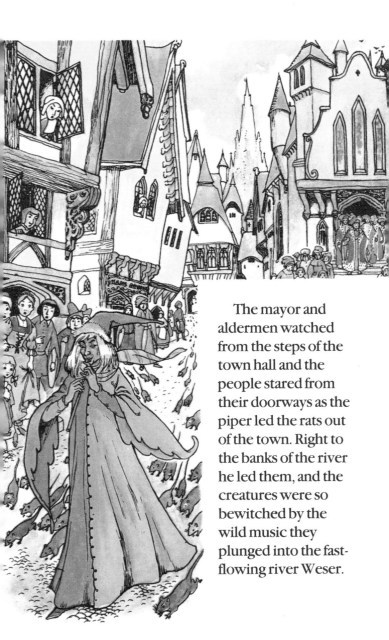

The mayor and aldermen watched from the steps of the town hall and the people stared from their doorways as the piper led the rats out of the town. Right to the banks of the river he led them, and the creatures were so bewitched by the wild music they plunged into the fast-flowing river Weser.

The people of
Hamelin gave a great
cheer to be rid of the
rats. Every bell in
every steeple rang
and the children
danced in the streets.
The mayor's face
beamed with pleasure
– until he saw the tall
figure of the Pied
Piper and
remembered his
bargain. He frowned.
Fifty thousand
guilders!

"My thousand guilders, please," said the Pied Piper.

"A thousand guilders to a wandering gypsy!" thought the mayor. "The rats are all drowned. He can't bring them back!"

"A thousand guilders!" he said to the piper.

"Come now, my good fellow, that was only a joke. I will give you fifty."

The gentle smile on the piper's face changed to a frown.

"If you cheat me," he said, "I shall play a different tune. One you won't like."

"You can play till you burst, for all I care!" said the mayor angrily, and paid him nothing.

The mayor and the people of Hamelin cared nothing for the Pied Piper now that they were rid of the rats.

Now that their worries were over, they were ready to make fun of the comical stranger. They laughed and pointed at him as he walked calmly out of the market-place.

The piper said nothing, but he lifted the pipe to his lips and started to play. It was a tune full of enchantment, the notes sweet and clear as a birdcall. To the horror of every grown-up person in Hamelin, the children started to stream out of the houses and follow the Pied Piper, leaping and laughing happily and clapping their hands. Tumbling and skipping and never taking their eyes from him, they followed the Pied Piper through the streets of Hamelin and out of the town towards the mountains. The sweet, enchanted music was for them alone and they could hear nothing else.

"Come back! Oh, please come back!" pleaded their mothers.

But they could not turn back. They were under a spell of enchantment that nothing could break. With hearts as heavy as stones, the parents watched as their children danced joyfully away.

They followed the piper through fields and over streams until they reached a mountain that rose high above the town. He led them to the opening of a cave and without a backward glance, all the children streamed in and the cave closed behind them for ever.

Well, not *all.* One little lame boy had not been able to keep up with his friends and was left behind. He turned sadly back to Hamelin where his parents wept for joy to see him, but he wept from sorrow.

He told them that the sweet notes of the magic pipe had told him about a wonderful country, more wonderful and beautiful than anyone could ever dream, where there was nothing but happiness, and where no one was ever sad or lame or tired.

As the years went by, other children were born in Hamelin, but no one could ever forget the story of the Pied Piper, and for one of the Hamelin churches, an artist made a window in coloured glass, showing the procession of little children following the tall figure of the Pied Piper.

Carnival
An imprint of Children's Division
of the Collins Publishing Group
8 Grafton Street, London W1X 3LA

Published by Carnival 1988

ISBN 0 00 194485 1

Printed & bound in Great Britain by
PURNELL BOOK PRODUCTION LIMITED
A MEMBER OF BPCC plc

HOPPER
COT